Table Talk

A
Maundy Thursday
Resource

Marion Fairman

CSS Publishing Company, Inc.
Lima, Ohio

TABLE TALK

ISBN 0-7880-0290-2

To the hungry ones of the world who come to the table of the Lord trusting they will, indeed, be fed.

Notes

- The material in *Table Talk* is prepared for three readers and the congregation.

- Permission is given to duplicate those portions of the material needed for outline clarification and for the response of the people.

- The Communion should be prepared and served as is customary in the church.

- All of the hymns suggested are well-known and are found in many hymnbooks. If desired, one or two anthems may be substituted for one or two hymns.

- Playing time:
    Speaking parts — 15 minutes
    Music — 20-25 minutes
    Communion service — 15-20 minutes
    Total time — 50-60 minutes

Table Talk

by Marion Fairman

I: **The Prayer**
"For The Bread Which Thou Hast Broken"

II: **At The Table Of The Pharisee**
"Just As I Am Without One Plea"

III: **At The Table Of Simon**
"What Shall I Render To The Lord?"

IV: **At The Table Of Levi**
"Oh Jesus, I Have Promised"

V: **At The Table Of Passover**
"Let Us Break Bread Together On Our Knees"

VI: **The Communion**

(When all is finished, Reader 1 comes forward to lead the response of the people)

Reader 1: Speak loud, speak clear! We have eaten the bread of the Lord!

People: We have eaten the bread of reconciliation — broken for all the world!

Reader 1: And we have drunk the wine of the Lord!

People: We have drunk the wine of love, poured out for all mankind. The bread of reconciliation, the wine of love is now within us!

Reader 1: How can we not be nourished by such bread and such wine?

People: Indeed! How can we not be strengthened in our faith, in our love, and in our understanding by the table talk of Jesus, our Lord?

Hymn: "Break Thou The Bread Of Life"

VII: The Benediction

Table Talk

(The Communion table is prepared and covered. The three readers may take their places during the prelude. Depending upon the structure of the area, arrange the three in a "rough" triangle — perhaps one at the pulpit, one at the lectern and one directly behind the communion table. Or, to center the focus on the communion table, one behind the table, one on each side of the table. Chairs or stools may be provided. Note: all music is simply suggested.)

Prelude: "Sacrament" from *St. Matthew's Passion* Bach

I: The Prayer

Reader 1: Oh God, this night is filled with somber memories and fearful hope. Let us remember.

Reader 3: When we remember that we are made of clay and that "all flesh is grass" *(Isaiah 37:27 KJV)*, we tremble. But when we also remember that You are known through the witness of the scriptures and the fellowship of bread broken and the cup shared, we rejoice.

Reader 2: May your presence fill this room as it filled that home in Emmaus when, in the breaking of bread, "their eyes were opened and they recognized Him" *(Luke 24:31)*.

Reader 1: As You accept us in the eating of bread and the drinking of wine, help us, at this table, to make the acceptance of ourselves and of each other complete — through Jesus Christ, our Lord. Amen.

Hymn: "For The Bread Which Thou Hast Broken"

II: At The Table Of The Pharisee

Reader 1: Have you ever wondered if you belonged at this table? Jesus, without hesitation, ate and drank with Gentile sinners, Jewish tax collectors, and law-driven Pharisees. This openness on the part of Jesus, this acceptance of others, this rebellion against social and religious barriers, shows us we too are welcome at the table of the Lord.

Reader 2: Have you ever thought what it means to offer food and to accept it from someone else? For one thing, sharing food implies recognition of another as a person like yourself. And because food is a necessity, to share it includes the acknowledgement of mutual need. Jesus, on this Thursday evening of Holy Week, imbued food with meaning; no wonder the sharing of bread and wine at the Last Supper has become central to our faith! Wherever Jesus ate, he talked — to friends, to enemies, and to disciples. Share tonight some table talk with Jesus.

Reader 3: One Sabbath, Jesus went to eat at the home of one of the leading Pharisees; people watched Jesus closely. During the meal, a man whose arms and legs were swollen came to Him. And Jesus spoke up and asked the teachers of the Law, "Does our Law allow healing on the Sabbath or not?"

But they would not say a thing. Jesus took the man, healed him and sent him away. Then he said to the Pharisees, "If any one of you had a son — or an ox — that happened to fall into a well on a Sabbath day, would you not pull him out at once?" And all were silent before Him *(Luke 14:1-6)*.

Reader 2: Why were the Pharisees — the whole crowd — watching Jesus so closely?

Reader 1: Oh — to see if Jesus would break the Sabbath laws.

Reader 3: Was everything covered by the Law of the Sabbath?

Reader 1: Everything! Even the food for the Sabbath meal had to be prepared the day before, and the meal itself was subject to a hundred regulations!

Reader 3: Yet, on that strict Sabbath, Jesus healed a man!

Reader 2: And never asked the man with the swollen arms if he had washed his hands in the manner prescribed by law!

Reader 3: At this table, Jesus rearranged people's priorities!

Reader 1: At this table, then, Jesus taught that regard for life, both physical and spiritual, comes before prescribed regulations. And the Pharisees could find no fault and sat silent before Him.

Hymn: "Just As I Am Without One Plea"

III: At The Table Of Simon

Reader 2: On another occasion, a Pharisee named Simon invited Jesus to have dinner with him. As He was resting on one arm to eat, a sinful woman brought an alabaster jar full of perfume and stood behind Jesus at his feet, crying and wetting his feet with her tears. Then she dried his feet with her hair, kissed them, and poured the perfume on them. When Simon saw this, he said to himself, "If this man really were a prophet, He would know who this woman is who is touching Him; He would know what kind of sinful life she leads."

Jesus spoke up and said to him, "Simon, I have something to tell you."

"Yes, Teacher," Simon said, "tell me."

"There were two men who owed money to a money lender," Jesus began. "One owed him five hundred silver coins, and the other man fifty. Neither of them could pay him back, so he canceled the debts of both. Which one will love him more?"

"I suppose," answered Simon grudgingly, "that it would be the one who was forgiven more."

"You are right," said Jesus. Then He turned to the woman and said to Simon. "Do you see this woman? I came into your house, and you gave me no water for my feet, but she has washed my feet with her hair. You did not welcome me with a kiss, but she has not stopped kissing my feet since I came. You provided no olive oil for my head, but she has covered my feet with perfume. I tell you, then, the great love she has shown proves that her many sins have been forgiven. But whoever has been forgiven little shows only a little love" *(Luke 7:36-47).*

Reader 1: Perhaps some here tonight do not know that, by custom, a Jewish host always placed his hands on a guest's shoulders and gave him the kiss of peace.

Reader 3: Or that because of the dusty roads, water was always poured over the guest's feet.

Reader 2: Yes — and a touch of perfumed oil placed on the guest's head to show him he was welcome.

Reader 3: None of these customary courtesies was performed by Simon, but poured out in love by the woman whom Jesus had forgiven.

Reader 2: We must hear Jesus' table talk accurately here. This woman is not forgiven because she loves; she loves Jesus because she has been forgiven!

Reader 3: At Simon's table, Jesus warns that those who reluctantly love Jesus have known little forgiveness. More than that, He teaches that salvation is by faith in Jesus Christ. Acts of love are not to earn salvation; they are expressions of gratitude for grace received.

Hymn: "What Shall I Render To The Lord?"

IV: At The Table Of Levi

Reader 1: One day Jesus saw a tax collector named Levi, sitting in his office. Jesus said to him, "Follow me." Levi, whom we know better as Matthew, got up, left everything, and followed Jesus. Later, Levi had a big feast in his house for Jesus; among the guests were a large number of the despised tax collectors and other common people. Some Pharisees and teachers of the Law complained to Jesus' disciples.

"Why do you eat and drink with tax collectors and other outcasts?" they asked.

But it was Jesus who answered them. "People who are well do not need a doctor, but only those who are sick. I have not come to call respectable people to repent, but outcasts" *(Luke 5:27-31)*.

Reader 3: Another time, Jesus was eating at the house of a Pharisee and told this parable. "There was once a man who was giving a great banquet to which he invited many people. When it was time for the feast, he sent his servants to tell his guests, 'Come, everything is ready!' But they all began, one after another, to make excuses.

The first one told the servant, 'I have bought a field and I must go and look at it; please accept my apologies.'

Another one said, 'I have bought five pairs of oxen and am on my way to try them out; please accept my apologies.'

Another one said, 'I have just gotten married, and for that reason I cannot come.'

The servant went back and told all this to the master. The master was furious and said to his servant, 'Hurry out to the streets and alleys of the town and bring back the poor, the crippled, the blind and the lame.'

Soon the servant returned and said, 'Your order has been carried out, Sir, but there is room for more.'

So the master said, 'Go out to the country roads and lanes and make people come in, so that my house will be full. I tell you that none of these persons who were invited will taste my dinner!' '' *(Luke 14:16-24).*

Reader 1: In both of these table stories, respectability and faith in Christ are equated, an idea that Jesus immediately strikes down as self-delusion.

Reader 2: At these tables, Jesus shows us that no one is ever excluded except by his own choice. But no one's reluctance or prejudice or stubbornness is permitted to ruin God's celebration!

Reader 3: Oh, Lord, may we never refuse the invitation to this — your table!

Hymn: "Oh, Jesus, I Have Promised"

V: At The Table Of Passover

Reader 1: On that Thursday evening of Holy Week that we are remembering, Jesus invited His disciples to eat the Passover with Him. They had scarcely begun the meal when an argument broke out around the table as to which one of them was the greatest of the disciples. Jesus said to them, "The kings of the pagans have power over their people . . . But this is not the way it is with you. Rather, the greatest one among you must be like the youngest, and the leader must be like the servant."

Then He poured some water into a washbasin and began to wash the disciples' feet *(Luke 22:24-26 and John 13:5).*

14

Reader 2: Imagine arguing about who was the greatest at the last supper they would eat with Jesus!

Reader 3: Right! But how many times do we think we're a bit better than those who come to church only at Easter and Christmas?

Reader 2: When Jesus began to wash the disciples' feet, we know how Peter reacted — all of them must have been filled with shame.

Reader 1: Oh, Lord — at your communion table as we examine our lives — we have known such shame.

Reader 3: Oh, Lord, at your communion table, show us how to be your faithful servants!

Reader 2: Later on that evening, Jesus said, "I tell you, one of you will betray me."

The disciples were very upset and began to ask Him, one after the other, "Surely, Lord, you don't mean me?"

Jesus answered, "One who dips his bread in the dish with me will betray me. The Son of Man will die as the scriptures say He will, but how terrible for that man who will betray me . . . !"

Judas, the traitor, spoke up. "Surely, Teacher, you don't mean me?" he asked. Jesus answered, "So you say" *(Matthew 26:20-25)*.

Reader 1: No matter how close we are to Jesus, we learn too soon what it means to be a Judas!

Reader 2: Lord, we need your forgiveness.

Reader 1: In the holiest of times, we can sin against you, Lord, and against one another —

Reader 2: Oh Lord, how we need your forgiveness!

Reader 1: In His holy table talk we see our own sin laid bare —

Together: *(passionately)* Lord! Forgive us and take away our shame!

Hymn: "Let Us Break Bread Together On Our Knees"

Reader 1: The table is prepared for us. Jesus, our Host, awaits those who will come. Brothers and sisters, let us join together in this holy communion!

VI: The Communion

(When all is finished, Reader 1 comes forward to lead the response of the people)

Reader 1: Speak loud, speak clear! We have eaten the bread of the Lord!

People: We have eaten the bread of reconciliation — broken for all the world!

Reader 1: And we have drunk the wine of the Lord!

People: We have drunk the wine of love, poured out for all mankind. The bread of reconciliation, the wine of love is now within us!

Reader 1: How can we not be nourished by such bread and such wine?

People: Indeed! How can we not be strengthened in our faith, in our love, and in our understanding by the table talk of Jesus, our Lord?

Hymn: "Break Thou The Bread Of Life"

VII: The Benediction